Copyright Information Page

Copyright © 2012 by Andy Hunt. All rights reserved worldwide.

No part of this publication may be replicated, redistributed, or given away in any form without the prior written consent of the author/publisher or the terms relayed to you herein.

Andy Hunt
andyhuntsales@gmail.com

Dedication

I dedicate this book to time. Sometimes speeding up, sometimes slowing down, sometimes a constraint we put upon ourselves.

Table of Contents

Copyright Information Page

Introduction

Chapter 1 - Get Good At Something

Chapter 2 - A Sales Career Goes Full Circle

    Stage 1 - Get Any Business

    Stage 2 - Do a Lot of Business

    Stage 3 - Go for Big Business

    Stage 4 - Full Circle Back to Any Business

Chapter 3 - Getting Non Price Sensitive Business

    Step 1 – Be Super Nice

    Step 2 – Do Your Job

    Step 3 – Know Something

Chapter 4 - Your List of Goals

    How to Set Those Goals

Chapter 5 - Never Take It Personally

    My Best Advice

Chapter 6 - Just Take the Phone Off The Hook

Chapter 7 - Don't Say Anything Stupid

Chapter 8 - In Closing

Index

About The Author

Introduction

In sales it pays to have a good memory. I can actually remember the day I was born: it was dark and then became light!

I was born into a sales family and this is where the basis for much of my practical experience came from; it is my pleasure to share this information with you. After all, that's what people want the most in the business world - information. Most books have very short introductions that go unread; however, I ask that you please read mine as it sets the basis for what I discuss. So, here we go...

At the earliest possible point in your career your main objective will be to develop as much *Non Price Sensitive Business* as possible. Later when you evaluate your customer's overall profitability index, you'll see that this type of business has allowed you to maximize the customer's lifetime value.

By changing the dynamics of your sales career you will become a business entity within yourself and become occupationally recession proof, finding work in good times and bad. My ideas and stories will give you the basic components for helping you to attract customers; that, in turn, will allow you to increase your income.

Anyone can sell price and a certain percentage of your business will be strictly based on price. However, if you sell price alone then your career with either be short or non-fulfilling. Always remember that *Non Price Sensitive Business* is the best, and this book will help you become a salesperson that uses your intelligence and imagination to sell something other than price.

It was through necessity that I had to go to work - I had no choice; at least that was what my father told me.

My first job at age 14 was working in the tobacco fields of Connecticut. This was a summertime job, and in the Connecticut Valley the summers are generally hot and humid, you get up at the crack of dawn and take the tobacco bus to the fields. Then you sit in the dirt and pick the tobacco leaves. Not much fun.

After two summers of that I realized for me personally a job under a roof is much better that a job in a field. For that matter – and to this day - I try to constantly rededicate myself to improve who I am, both professionally and personally.

My first job indoors was working as a salesperson at a steel service center; it took me a full sixteen years before I was promoted into management. Initially, I started part time, worked my way up to being employed full time and for more than 10 years I was the number one salesperson in the office.

When I was promoted into management, I finally and fully realized that I enjoyed training people; it was here that I was making a difference in the lives of others. In my heart and soul I truly enjoy making this difference; and this is why I am here, partnering with you in an effort to try to better your life and the lives of others.

Also, within this book I discuss how you can learn to provide your customers with *Super Personal Business Service*. These are basic sales fundamentals that will increase your productivity and make your job easier and fun.

In the offices we work in we all notice that some salespeople achieve better than others. Why?

Why is there a difference in one person's output when compared to another person? What is this difference?

This book offers basic ideas that put you in the direction of being that top performer. Always remember it is you and your attitude that will allow you to become that top performer. Thanks for reading my book!

Chapter 1 - Get Good At Something

So you're starting that new career. That's right, it is a career! Never think of it as a job, always as a career. In this day and age we must work, and unless you're incredibly wealthy, you'll need to make a good living. If you're already wealthy, well then you somehow did something smart to get there. As the saying goes, we all have to "*put bread on the table.*"

It's interesting how successful people get their start in their new career. By calling it a career, rather than a mere job, you'll build up volumes of self-esteem and confidence.

Here is a quick tip, one you can get good at right away: when speaking in business dealings, <u>be confident</u>; end your sentences with periods, not question marks. Don't speak in a halting manner, just be yourself and show confidence. It doesn't matter if you're new or uncertain of yourself, project confidence. A potential customer or client doesn't need to know that you've just started working at this new career of yours.

My first career was working as an inside salesperson for over 25 years in the steel industry. At the point in my life when I got that job I really wasn't career minded.

It was back in 1979 and I was in my junior year of high school. I was in a business math class for high school students involved in the after school work education program. The teacher asked the class "*Would anyone want a job at a steel company?*"

For whatever reason I put up my hand, I was the only one who did so. Why did I want to work at this steel company? What did I, a 16-year-old know about metal?

In 9th grade I did okay in wood shop and had gotten a passing grade. However, that same year I also had failed metal shop. I failed it with a big fat *F grade*.

You have to understand that I come from a highly non-mechanical family. It was a big deal that I could change a tire on a car. Heck it was a big deal that I could wash a car. That aside, why was I going to work at a steel company?

In 10th grade I had taken welding class. My high school had wonderful welding facilities and that, coupled with some outstanding teachers, helped to ensure my success in that class. I took it for both semesters that year and enjoyed it.

For whatever reason at that young age it struck me as totally interesting to learn about the periodic table of elements. In general the carbon content of steel determines the weldability of metal, so when I was 15 I set out to learn anything and everything about the carbon content of steel.

So here I am in March 1979, walking into the steel company for my very first interview. It was a standing interview, and it lasted a solid two minutes - I got the job! This started on April 1st; yes, April fool's Day 1979.

It was an easy job, and the steel orders came either by phone or U.S Mail. The orders that came in the mail were these incredibly long tedious orders for 40 or 50 or 80 items. I was given one of these orders per day. This is another thing I quickly *got good at*.

As my business day was only from 2 to 5 p.m., I developed the habit of working at a very high rate of speed. The senior salespeople I worked with wanted nothing to do with these time consuming orders. So I got very good at doing them.

Also, the steel company gave me small amounts of scrap steel to take home to weld. I had bought an arc welder with my spare money and had set up a small welding shop at my home. The hours I spent on this hobby enabled me to relate first hand with customers about the weld ability of certain alloy steels. With the exception of my folks praying that I didn't burn the house down with all the welding sparks, it was a win-win situation.

Okay, so that was a good story about how I got started. You'd imagine after doing that line of work for a number of years, I knew it quite well. So it was time for a change. I asked myself can I do it in two different careers?

I had the bright idea in 2005 to quit my job in the steel industry and move to North Myrtle Beach, South Carolina.

Now let me tell you, North Myrtle Beach is a wonderful place. The weather is great and the beach is wide and long and the folks there are genuinely nice, I can't wait to see all of you there again, "*y'all*".

After sitting around for a few weeks and getting bored I went to a local real estate seminar and was impressed. So I jumped right into real estate school and by April 2006 had become a Realtor.

So, after this, I'm in North Myrtle Beach, South Carolina and I know two people. How the heck am I going to sell a home?

I know, I've got to *get good at something*.

To meet people I did open houses; on every Saturday and Sunday, and some weekdays as well. I think I did 178 open houses in two years, and the people I met at those open houses in May 2006 resulted in four closings; this is pretty good for a new agent in the marketplace.

What happened to me the first time I had floor time - the first call I got - is that I sold those folks a home. It was a Friday afternoon, and I got one call about 2PM; it was from a prospect looking to view a home. I got to the house about 45 minutes after their phone call, and opened the front door for the couple to go in.

As I was opening the door, the wife yelled "*I want it*!" It was a cash sale, and 12 days after I showed them the home I had my commission check. Sweet!

All you have to do it get good at something. It's that easy. Be that *go to* person that your office needs. Many times when your talent comes out, you're recognized and doors open up for you; the possibilities are there.

When I was a young child, I'd play with my toy trucks out in the yard or in the sandbox. Once my mom asked me what I wanted to be. I told her a garbage man on a garbage truck. That might be my next career.

Chapter 2 - A Sales Career Goes Full Circle

So, you've gotten that job in sales that you were looking for - outstanding work on your part! What is the focus of your job? In sales it is to produce.

The easiest path for me to follow has been to set goals and objectives and then try to meet or beat them.

Essentially here is the *Full Circle Sales Path* that you will take.

- Stage 1 - Get Any Business
- Stage 2 - Do a Lot of Business
- Stage 3 - Go for Big Business
- Stage 4 - Full Circle Back to Any Business

Stage 1 - Get Any Business

The first thing you are looking for when you've first started that new career is to get any business; you want - **and need** - that first sale, or that first order.

You don't care how or why it comes your way, and you're so excited and full of energy!

As a new or junior salesperson you should be willing and able to tackle whatever is thrown your way. Many times your company may give you contentious or difficult to handle customers to start.

What this really means is that others within the company don't want to work as hard as it will take to get this business. However you're new, you'll do whatever it takes.

Treat the situation like a "*real one*", provide excellent service, treat the customer with respect, and you'll get their business. Furthermore, the customers will also like you.

Guess what? You **are** *getting the business* and you are now on your way.

Stage 2 - Do a Lot of Business

The next stage in your business career path is to attempt to get *a lot of business*. You've had a quick start, received your first few orders and rounds of business, and have shown that you do have the sales skills needed; you also have aptitude - now you want a lot of business.

Everyone knows you're now willing to take anything thrown your way. This then gives you the opportunity to crank up your speed and your accuracy rate; and, before you know it you will be starting to pull away from your other sales peers and *doing a lot of business*.

Stage 3 - Go for Big Business

It takes many sales people years to get to the point of only wanting to handle big business.

You've climbed the sales mountain, you're looking out at the vastness of it all; and congratulations, you are handling the top 10 percent of the company's business. When you speak, people listen to you, and your sentences and manner show your confidence. It is a good feeling to have made it to the Big Business stage but always remember that big customers bring big problems.

I always judge a company by the way they handle their problems. My best advice to you is to always try to handle any problem situation as <u>promptly as possible</u>.

No matter how big or small the problem, your reaction time shows that you care and have the ability to provide *Super Personal Business Service* and can *go for big business*.

Stage 4 - Full Circle Back to Any Business

Of course, it depends upon what type of business you're in; and it is likely that these four business paths can take months or years. However, the hard work has paid off and customers are now telling you are that they are thankful for your *Super Personal Business Service*.

Slowly you've turned from selling price into selling service; people want to deal with you **because of who you are.**

You're now starting to handle *Non Price Sensitive Business* and, just like when you started, you'll take any business. The sales theory behind this is that with any business, as long as it is provided with your *Super Personal Business Service*, it will lead to the desired end result of a combination of big business, small business, quality referrals and your sales lifestyle becoming more enjoyable.

Any part of the sales circle is exciting!

As they say on the bottle of hair shampoo: *rinse-lather-repeat.*

In your sales career you can mix these techniques up a bit; the actual technique used, depends on what part of the business cycle you're in.

Congratulations, you've just come *full circle*.

Chapter 3 - Getting Non Price Sensitive Business

Here is a question for you, as a salesperson, *"How much of your business is non-price sensitive?"*

Wait, how can I ask such a silly question? Can business really be non-price sensitive? The answer to this is yes, it can.

Here are three simple basic ideas on how you can increase your *Non Price Sensitive Business*:

1. Be Super Nice
2. Do Your Job
3. Know Something

Step 1 – Be Super Nice

Let me say that again - *be super nice*. If you are going to be in direct sales or telephone sales, then you must be a super nice person while working. It doesn't matter what your job is, be it retail or at a call center or the restaurant trade or any job where you provide a service or represent something for sale.

These words, in a sincere and polite nature, must be in your sales vocabulary:

- Hello
- Good morning
- Good afternoon
- Thank you
- Have a good day
- May I help you?
- How is your family doing?
- Did you enjoy your weekend?
- Thank you for your business
- Thank you for being such a valuable customer all these years
- Thank you for your valuable time

As far as making any type of comment about the way a person looks, it is best to say, *"...and you're looking well today."*

Another good practice when you are speaking on the phone is to try and say the customer's name back to them; people love to hear their own name – and it shows you are being attentive and emphasizes the personal touch.

Similarly, ensure the tone changes in your voice when talking (at the appropriate time, of course), don't be stale or monotonous - this indicates boredom and is the last thing you want to imply.

If you are writing e-mails, you can show the same style with your writing. You must do this every day or else you're in the wrong line of work.

Don't overdo any of these, just be attentive, offer good service and *be super nice*.

Step 2 – Do Your Job

Be sure to do your job.

You need to provide excellent service, and follow up when required. I gained recognition in the business world by responding quickly.

In my opinion the promptness of the response will win you a certain percentage of business just because you are responding quickly. Customers will learn to trust you. Determine the customer's wants and needs, describe your benefits, differentiate your offerings from your competition and always do a quick concise summary.

When needed I also enjoy giving a customer a choice on what product to buy; many buyers like it if you offer product comparisons – as well as *doing your job*, you're making their job easier.

Step 3 – Know Something

You must *know something* about your customer, and show interest in them - know their interests. Be it their hobbies, sports, travel, weather, food, their kids or family or whatever else they enjoy. If you can make business secondary in the conversation, but still important, then you are on your way to forming *Non Price Sensitive Business* relationships.

I send customers newspaper clippings, a cartoon from the funny pages, a horoscope on a birthday, sports stories, a thank you note, to show a personal interest and appreciation of the customer. Sorry, I'm not a big junk e-mail sender to my customers of videos of pets bouncing basketballs and things of that nature.

To get business you must eliminate the unknown variables of concern to potential customers. Of course these unknowns may include price, delivery, and any other variable that may apply. Once you eliminate these variables you are able to mix up your closing sales techniques with your Non Price Sensitive smoozing.

We have to take what we can from life, be friendly, and be informed, have a sense of humor and, most of all, care. If you show you care, truly care, then over time the percentage of your *Non Price Sensitive Business* will increase! You can make great gains just by *knowing something* more about your customer.

Again I ask you, what percentage of your business is Non Price Sensitive?

Chapter 4 - Your List of Goals

Goals basically motivate us within our business environment. Personally, I have greater job satisfaction when I meet my own goals, and I feel empowered as an employee.

After a few months in sales I started to make a list of my goals. I was keeping track of my daily sales, which then became monthly and yearly numbers. Sales trends that shape my business landscape interest me, and over time you could learn to justify a slow or, for that matter, a busy business cycle.

For example, traditional school vacation weeks were always slow, as was the summer period. In contrast though, months such as March - with twenty three-business days - are always big volume months.

Prior to this, I never considered myself a truly competitive person; yet, all of a sudden, I was into trends and sales performance. This led me to becoming a goal-orientated salesperson and committed to my sales goals.

Whenever business was slow or I was having a personally slow time, I would rededicate myself to a set of new or similar goals. To this day I constantly rededicate myself in an effort to improve who I am both professionally and personally.

How to Set Those Goals

The easiest way for me to do this is to write down ten goals that I have.

After I write them down, I number them in the order of importance; this is the part where you come in. These goals can be something easy, some business matter that just doesn't want to go away, or it could be something simple that you really want to get done. When it's accomplished, say in the next day or two, you cross it off your list and move onto items two through ten.

You'll see that mixing up some short term goals along with some long term goals will professionally lead to the best results. Sometimes it will seem like you're running into walls; but, by listing your professional goals - and for that matter I even do it with personal goals - you will get that feeling of accomplishment. I always date these lists as this enables me to go back and review it after a few months; I can then make a new list.

You can also use it as a tool by showing your supervisors that you made your list, accomplished some of the objectives and are moving onto the next set of objectives. By doing so you may very well hear your supervisor say the words we all want to hear; *"What can we do to help you meet your next set of goals?"*

If you're ever having a problem with the goals, say to yourself; *"I can do whatever I want, I'm **[insert your full name here]***". Try it, it works!

Chapter 5 - Never Take It Personally

I try to keep this book as funny and upbeat as possible, but still I wanted to cover a bit of a serious topic. Have your ever heard the saying; *"If you can't take a joke, you shouldn't be in the business."*? It's something that I've heard often, and in jest, in many business situations.

Some of the best advice I can ever offer is to never take situations in the business world personally.

I came from a real estate family. My parents had their own successful real estate business in a small suburban town for more than twenty five years. To have success in the real estate business you have to know people, a lot of people, and my folks knew everyone.

As I mentioned, our family valued our time together and every night we'd get together at our dinner table at 6PM. We all made it a point as best we could NOT to talk about business at dinner; this was family time, and was a time to relax.

After 20 or 25 minutes, I would sneak away from the table to feed the dog, the cats, and do my other chores; while doing these, I would often hear my Dad saying to my Mom; *"You're taking this business situation too personally Eleanor."*

My mom was an outstandingly smart salesperson and she wanted so hard to achieve in the business world. At times, she could not understand why she'd be having particular problems with a customer, or maybe even lose a deal that she had going with some of her close friends, a neighbor, or a golfing buddy.

Nevertheless, this is the nature of the business and sometimes, due to some hidden element, things would go wrong and the deal would collapse.

Ahh, but this is just human nature. How do you not take business personally?

It is easy to say it, but it is just a *state of mind*.

Yes, we want to achieve; Yes, we have objectives; Yes, we have to put bread on the table - we all have mouths to feed; but just because they don't want to deal with you, or buy that widget from you, it doesn't make it personal, so don't take it personally.

There are other factors in that person's life that we can't possibly know about, and these will have led them to their decision, and caused them to act or react in the manner that they have. You didn't anticipate it and, quite frankly, it would be nigh on impossible for anyone to have done so – *so don't take it personally.*

Once I was traveling on the road visiting my customers and having a very productive day. I arrived for a 1:30PM meeting and, on this occasion, was kept waiting. After 30 minutes had gone by I was told; *"We are sorry we just don't have time to see you today."*

So what did I do? What could I do?

I smiled politely, said thank you, got in my car and went to my next appointment.

I did my best to shrug off what I sensed as negative sales karma; but, still I felt a bit down. It wasn't my fault the appointment got cancelled, but I'm sure they had their reasons. However, I kept my cool, I was polite, I didn't get angry – that's business.

Interestingly enough, starting later that day (and continuing for the next few months) I got more quotes and orders from that particular customer than I ever did before – all because *I didn't take it personally*.

My Best Advice

If you're at home at night and unable to sleep, as a business deal is keeping you up wondering about it, then I suggest you repeat this to yourself; *"I am calm, cool and tranquil, and I will succeed at everything I do tomorrow."*

Chapter 6 - Just Take the Phone Off The Hook

When I was growing up, we had two traditional rotary dial phones in our house. One was attached on the wall, and the other was in my parent's home office.

For a half an hour every night, while we were eating dinner, these phones were taken "off the hook". We needed to have family time and my dad's thinking was that if it was important the caller would phone back.

I work so hard during the business day that nothing gets me more upset than a phone ringing when I'm having dinner.

No, wait, there is something!

It's a person texting or instant messaging at the dinner table.

What are you going to miss in this half an hour, this 30 minutes, this 1800 seconds that cannot wait?

Tell me now; I'm listening because its 2PM. and I'm not eating dinner!

If I'm out to lunch with a customer, or in a meeting, my cell phone is turned off. These folks are going out of their way to spend time with me, and I give them the utmost personal attention.

In a business sense we have lost the art of personal communication, and that is what business is all about, that personal, professional touch.

Give it a try at home with your family, when having dinner, turns off the phones, the TV's and talk. You and your family deserve that half of an hour peace and quiet!

Chapter 7 - Don't Say Anything Stupid

We all cause our own problems and can be our own worst enemies. We all say some really dumb things sometime and it seems that every day there is a news story about someone who has stuck their foot in their mouth.

It does happen, but try - and I mean try - to not let it happen at work. When at work we have to be on our best business behavior. It's not easy but let's gives it a try.

What is the best way to do this?

It means *think before you speak.*

If your company has a policy manual you should read it. It's there to protect you and others from what the company deems as improper behavior. We live in a litigious society and at times what you may perceive as a funny joke may actually offend someone. The French expression *'faux pas'* means a violation of accepted social norms.

One of the greatest co-workers I ever had called me with a problem. At the time, I was an inside sales manager, and he was the outside sales manager and he had to relay a situation he had just created to me.

It was mid-afternoon on a rainy Monday and he said, "I went to a large corporate account, and prior to my appointment with my internal company contact, was greeted by their support person."

"The support person asked me how I was doing, and for some reason - maybe it was the dreary weather - I said '*It was a good day for a murder.*' The next thing you know I was escorted out of the building and my appointment was cancelled."

Wow!

At that moment, while I was listening to my co-worker, I was told that the owner of that actual company was on the other line wanting to speak to me.

I took the call and listened as the owner of the company said, "*Don't have that salesperson of yours ever come to our company again. As long as he doesn't come back, we will continue to do business, just make sure he doesn't come back.*"

Of course, all I could say was "*Yes.*"

Now that was an extreme situation but my best advice, is to always "*stay on message.*" If by unfortunate chance you do say something that you regret - especially it has caused some type of business distress - the best thing to do is to deal with it quickly.

A smart business person addresses issues and problems without hesitation, and helps to eliminate any issue that might be interpreted as a negative.

Chapter 8 - In Closing

Andy's Sales Tips

I'd like to offer you these basic suggestions, handy sayings and ideas you can keep in your mind. When you're having a trying day, I hope that one of these affirmations can make your day a little better:

- Customer satisfaction means customer retention.
- Never ask the customer why they are in a hurry, that's their business.
- If you can't take a joke you shouldn't be in the business.
- Always treat every business situation like a real one.
- Any consummated business deal should be put in writing.
- Never take it personal.
- Always say what you know.
- Speak with confidence.
- Say their name.
- Elimination of variables allows you to close the deal.
- Ask for their business.

- Be able to answer the question. *"This is what I do best at my job."*
- Have a plan - don't let your plan be no plan.
- Get a good quality professional photo of yourself on the Internet.
- You work so hard to earn money; spend a little, save a little.

Now that you've read my book I have all the confidence in the world in you. The business world is waiting for you.

You have the skills, the ability, the sales vision and the know-how; but, most importantly, you have your mind – it is your mind that will inspire your natural sales ability to come out, and is the only thing standing in your way from becoming that outstanding success.

Assume and know your feeling of sales empowerment and use your *Super Personal Business Service* to go out and make your *Non Price Sensitive Business* happen!

Index
Customer's Lifetime Value.
Non Price Sensitive Business.
North Myrtle Beach.
Periodic Table.
Promoted into management.
South Carolina.
State of mind.
Stay on message.
Steel industry.
Super Personal Business Service.

About The Author

Andy Hunt has been in sales on the east coast of the USA since 1979.

Starting his career at age 16, he has gained valuable insight into business relationships and what makes them work.

As the number one salesperson for many years, his goal as a speaker and a sales mentor is to help make you into the best salesperson you can be.

Follow Andy on Twitter @leighandrewhunt or e-mail him at <andyhuntsales@gmail.com>

www.ingramcontent.com/pod-product-compliance
Lightning Source LLC
Chambersburg PA
CBHW070724180526
45167CB00004B/1602